Maiasaura

by Daniel Cohen

Consultant:
Larry Dean Martin, Ph.D.
Professor-Senior Curator
Natural History Museum and Biodiversity Research Center
University of Kansas, Lawrence, Kansas

Bridgestone Books
an imprint of Capstone Press
Mankato, Minnesota

Bridgestone Books are published by Capstone Press
151 Good Counsel Drive, P.O. Box 669, Mankato, Minnesota 56002
www.capstonepress.com

Library of Congress Cataloging-in-Publication Data
Cohen, Daniel, 1936–
    Maiasaura / by Daniel Cohen.
    p. cm.—(Discovering dinosaurs)
    Summary: Describes what is known about the physical characteristics, behavior, and habitat
of this plant-eating dinosaur.
    Includes bibliographical references and index.
    ISBN 0-7368-2522-3 (hardcover)
    1. Maiasaura—Juvenile literature. [1. Maiasaura. 2. Dinosaurs.] I.Title.
QE862.O65C62 2003
567.914—dc21   2003010804

Editorial Credits
Amanda Doering, editor; Linda Clavel, series designer; Enoch Peterson, book designer and
    illustrator; Alta Schaffer, photo researcher; Karen Risch, product planning editor

Photo Credits
Chris Butler/SPL/Photo Researchers Inc, 6
Michael F. Shores, 16
Museum of the Rockies, cover, 1, 10; Bruce Selyem, 20
The Natural History Museum, 14; Orbis, 4, 12
Rich Penney, www.dinosaur-man.com, 8

1 2 3 4 5 6 09 08 07 06 05 04

Table of Contents

Maiasaura compared to a
5-foot (1.5-meter) tall human

Maiasaura

Maiasaura (my-ah-SORE-ah) was a large plant-eating **dinosaur**. It lived more than 65 million years ago. Maiasaura was 30 feet (9 meters) long. It weighed 7,000 pounds (3,200 kilograms). Maiasaura means "good mother reptile."

The World of Maiasaura

Earth was different during maiasaura's time. The climate was warmer and wetter than it is today. Maiasaura lived in what is now North America.

climate
the usual weather in a place

Parasaurolophus

Relatives of Maiasaura

Maiasaura belonged to a group of dinosaurs called hadrosaurs (HAD-ro-sores). Hadrosaurs are also called duck-billed dinosaurs. Parasaurolophus (PAR-ah-sore-OL-o-fus) was a hadrosaur that lived during the time of maiasaura.

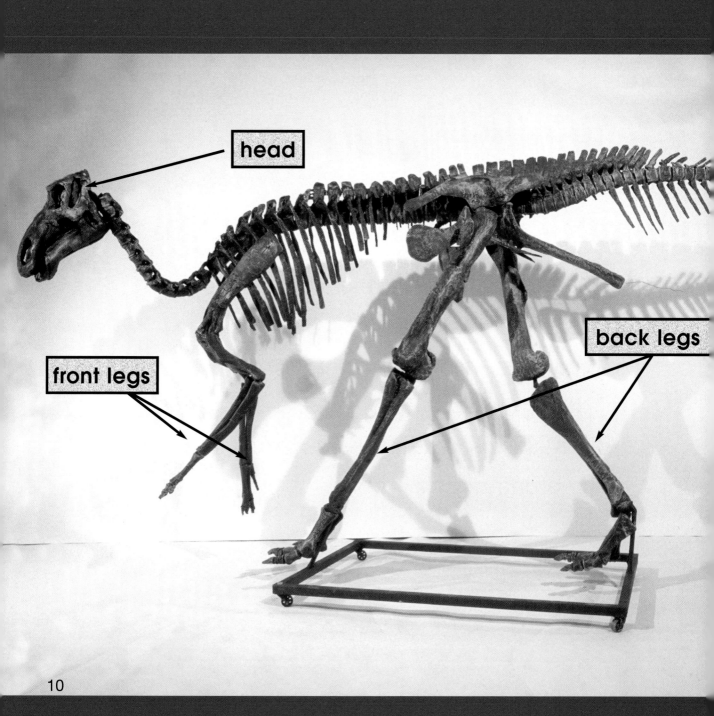

tail

Parts of Maiasaura

Maiasaura was 6 to 8 feet (1.8 to 2.4 meters) tall. It sometimes walked only on its strong back legs. Maiasaura had three toes on its back feet. It had four toes on its front feet. Maiasaura used its long, thick tail to **balance** its body.

What Maiasaura Ate

Maiasaura was a **herbivore**. It ate plants. It used its bony beak to tear off leaves. Maiasaura's jaws held about 150 ridged teeth. These teeth chopped and crushed plants. New teeth grew in place of worn ones.

Dromaeosaurus

Predators

Maiasaura did not have sharp teeth or claws to protect itself from predators. Large meat-eating dinosaurs ate maiasaura. Smaller dinosaurs like dromaeosaurus (drom-AY-oh-SORE-us) may have eaten maiasaura eggs.

predator
an animal that hunts and eats other animals

End of Maiasaura

Maiasaura and all other dinosaurs became **extinct** 65 million years ago. Many **scientists** believe a giant meteorite hit Earth. The effects of this meteorite may have killed the dinosaurs.

meteorite

a rock from space that falls to Earth

CANADA

Montana

UNITED STATES

MEXICO

Discovering Maiasaura

In 1978, Jack Horner and Bob Makela discovered a maiasaura nesting site in Montana. The nests were mounds about 7 feet (2 meters) wide. **Fossils** of 15 young maiasaura were also found. A few years later, more nests were found nearby.

Studying Maiasaura Today

Scientists learn many things from maiasaura nests. Scientists once thought baby dinosaurs took care of themselves. But around the nests, scientists found maiasaura fossils of different ages. Mother dinosaurs may have fed and cared for their young until they were adults.

Hands On: Measuring a Maiasaura Nest

Maiasaura nests were very large. They measured 6 to 10 feet (1.8 to 3 meters) wide. Try this activity to see how big a maiasaura nest was.

What You Need

3 friends
1 large ball of string

What You Do

1. Find a large area of grass or floor.
2. Have two friends lie on the grass or floor, head to head.
3. Tuck the end of the string under the feet of a person lying down to secure the string.
4. Have a friend help you roll out the string and shape a circle around the two people lying down.
5. When the circle is complete, have the two people lying down carefully get up, making sure not to disturb the string.
6. Look at the circle that has been made. It is the size of a maiasaura nest. How does it compare in size to a bird's nest?

Glossary

balance (BAL-uhnss)—to try to keep steady without falling

dinosaur (DYE-na-sore)—an extinct land reptile; dinosaurs lived on Earth for at least 150 million years.

extinct (ek-STINGKT)—no longer living anywhere in the world

fossil (FOSS-uhl)—the remains or traces of something that once lived; bones and footprints can be fossils.

herbivore (HUR-buh-vor)—an animal that eats only plants

scientist (SYE-uhn-tist)—a person who studies the world around us

Read More

Gray, Susan H. *Maiasaura.* Exploring Dinosaurs. Chanhassen, Minn.: Child's World, 2004.

Penner, Lucille Recht. *Dinosaur Babies.* Step Into Reading. New York: Random House, 2003.

Schomp, Virginia. *Maiasaura: And Other Duck-Billed Plant-Eaters.* Prehistoric World. New York: Benchmark Books, 2004.

Internet Sites

FactHound offers a safe, fun way to find Internet sites related to this book. All of the sites on FactHound have been researched by our staff.

Here's how:
1. Visit *www.facthound.com*
2. Type in this special code **0736825223** for age-appropriate sites. Or enter a search word related to this book for a more general search.
3. Click on the **Fetch It** button.

FactHound will fetch the best sites for you!

Index